First Facts™

From Farm to Table

From Milk to Cheese

by Roberta Basel

Consultant:
Art Hill, Professor of Food Science
University of Guelph
Guelph, Ontario, Canada

Capstone
press
Mankato, Minnesota

First Facts is published by Capstone Press,
151 Good Counsel Drive, P.O. Box 669, Mankato, Minnesota 56002.
www.capstonepress.com

Library of Congress Cataloging-in-Publication Data
Basel, Roberta.
From milk to cheese / by Roberta Basel.
    p. cm.—(First facts. From farm to table)
    Includes bibliographical references (p. 23) and index.
    Summary: "An introduction to the basic concept of food production, distribution,
and consumption by tracing the production of cheese from milk to the finished
product" —Provided by publisher.
    ISBN-13: 978-0-7368-4285-3 (hardcover)   ISBN-10: 0-7368-4285-3 (hardcover)
    1. Cheese making—Juvenile literature. 2. Cheese—Juvenile literature. I. Title. II. Series.
SF271.B355 2006
637.3—dc22   2004029195

Editorial Credits
Jennifer Besel, editor; Jennifer Bergstrom, set designer; Ted Williams, book designer;
    Wanda Winch, photo researcher/photo editor

Photo Credits
Capstone Press/Karon Dubke, cover, 1, 5, 19, 21
Comstock, back cover
Corbis/James Marshall, 14–15
David R. Frazier Photolibrary, 10–11, 16–17
Grant Heilman Photography Inc./Grant Heilman, 8, 12–13/Larry Lefever, 6
Kirby, Smith & Wilkins, 20
Unicorn Stock Photos/Eric R. Berndt, 9

1 2 3 4 5 6 10 09 08 07 06 05

Table of Contents

Say Cheese!

Cheese can be a tasty treat. Some people melt cheese on food, such as pizza. Other people eat cheese in slices or with crackers.

Cheese has to be made before people can eat it. Making cheese takes many steps.

Fun Fact!
Each person in the United States eats about 30 pounds (14 kilograms) of cheese each year.

It Starts with Milk

Most cheese is made from cow's milk. Cows make milk to feed their calves. Some cows make more milk than their calves need. People use the extra milk to make other foods, like cheese.

Fun Fact!
Some people make cheese from the milk of camels, goats, sheep, and reindeer.

From Cow to Factory

Farmers use **machines** to get milk from cows. The milk is pumped through pipes to large tanks. These tanks keep the milk cold.

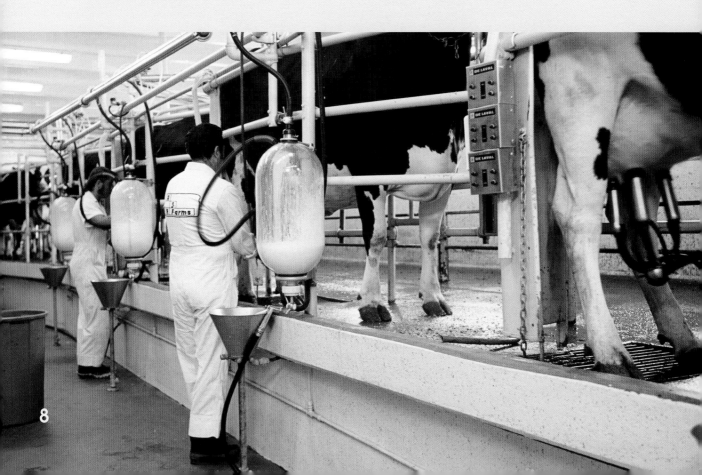

The milk is pumped from the tanks into trucks. Trucks take the milk to **factories**. There, the milk is made into cheese.

Making Curds

At the cheese factory, the milk is heated to kill **germs**. People add **bacteria** and **enzymes** to the milk. Bacteria and enzymes give the cheese its taste. They also make the milk form lumps, called **curds**. The liquid around the curds is called **whey**.

Fun Fact!
In the nursery rhyme, Little Miss Muffet ate curds and whey. Today, we call it cottage cheese.

Pressing

The curds are taken out of the whey and put into **molds**. Weights are pressed down on the molds. The curds become blocks or wheels of cheese.

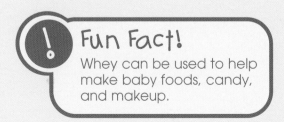

Fun Fact!
Whey can be used to help make baby foods, candy, and makeup.

Ripening

After the cheese is formed, it is taken out of the mold. The cheese is put in a storage room, where it **ripens**. Ripening gives the cheese its smell, flavor, and feel.

Some kinds of cheeses ripen for a few months. Other cheeses ripen for over a year.

Fun Fact!
Swiss cheese gets its holes while it ripens. Gases in the curds make the holes.

To the Store

When the cheese is ripe, it is sold. Factories sell cheese to many kinds of stores.

Workers put the cheese on airplanes, trucks, or trains. The cheese is kept cold on the way to the stores.

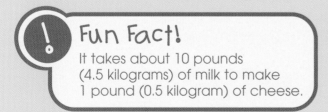

Fun Fact!
It takes about 10 pounds (4.5 kilograms) of milk to make 1 pound (0.5 kilogram) of cheese.

WHEELS

WHEELS

WHEELS

WHEELS

WHEELS

CATERPILLAR 35

17

Where to Find Cheese

Cheese is sold almost everywhere food is sold. Grocery stores sell many kinds of cheese, such as cheddar and Swiss. Gas stations and other small stores also sell cheese. Some people even make their own cheese at home.

Fun Fact!

People in Greece eat more cheese than people in any other country.

Amazing but True!

A giant cheddar cheese was made in 1964 for the New York World's Fair. The cheese weighed 38,080 pounds (17,273 kilograms). The cheese was carried across the United States in a large truck. Today, you can see the truck and a copy of the giant cheese in Neillsville, Wisconsin.

Hands On: Cheese Ball

You can use different kinds of cheeses to make a cheese ball. Ask an adult to help you with this activity.

What You Need

measuring cups and spoons
16 ounces (455 grams) cream cheese
¾ cup (180 mL) crumbled blue cheese
1 cup (240 mL) shredded sharp cheddar cheese
½ cup (120 mL) minced onion
1 tablespoon (15 mL) Worcestershire sauce
medium-sized mixing bowl
mixing spoon or electric mixer
crackers

What You Do

1. Use measuring cups to measure the cheeses.
2. Put the cheeses, onion, and Worcestershire sauce into the bowl.
3. Mix them together. You may want to use an electric mixer.
4. When everything is mixed, use your hands to shape the mixture into a ball.
5. Put your cheese ball in the refrigerator. Let it chill for eight hours. Then enjoy your cheese ball with crackers.

Glossary

bacteria (bak-TIHR-ee-uh)—tiny living things

curd (KURD)—the solid part of sour milk after the bacteria and enzymes have been added

enzyme (EN-zime)—a protein made by living cells

factory (FAK-tuh-ree)—a building where products are made in large numbers

germs (JURMS)—small living things that can make you sick

machine (muh-SHEEN)—a piece of equipment that is used to do a job

mold (MOHLD)—a shaped container

ripen (RYE-pen)—to become ready to be eaten

whey (WAY)—the watery part of milk

Read More

Klingel, Cynthia, and Robert B. Noyed. *Milk and Cheese.* Let's Read about Food. Milwaukee: Weekly Reader Early Learning Library, 2002.

Zemlicka, Shannon. *From Milk to Cheese.* Start to Finish. Minneapolis: Lerner, 2004.

Internet Sites

FactHound offers a safe, fun way to find Internet sites related to this book. All of the sites on FactHound have been researched by our staff.

Here's how:
1. Visit *www.facthound.com*
2. Type in this special code **0736842853** for age-appropriate sites. Or enter a search word related to this book for a more general search.
3. Click on the **Fetch It** button.

FactHound will fetch the best sites for you!

Index